The Tomb of Simon de Montfort

An Enquiry

David Cox

Published in Great Britain in 2019 by the Simon de Montfort Society with the kind consent of the Worcestershire Archaeological Society.

ISBN: 978-0-244-48052-3

© D C Cox

All rights reserved. Apart from any fair dealing for the purpose of private study, research, criticism or review, as permitted under the Copyright, Designs and Patents Act, 1988, no part of this publication may be reproduced, stored in a retrieval system, or transmitted in any form or by any means, electronic, electrical, chemical, mechanical, optical, photocopying, recording or otherwise, without the prior written permission of the copyright owner. Enquiries should be addressed to the publishers.

www.simondemontfort.org

Foreword

Until his retirement Dr David Cox, FSA, was county editor of the Victoria History of Shropshire and a lecturer at Keele University, and he is currently the 'go-to man' (to coin a phrase) on Evesham abbey and the Vale. Author of *The Church and Vale of Evesham, 700-1215: Lordship, Landscape and Prayer*, published in 2015, there is no-one with a greater knowledge of, and insight into, the structure, organisation and operation of the abbey of St Mary and St Ecgwine, more commonly known as Evesham abbey.

The fate of the remains of the earl of Leicester has long been a mystery. One foot of the dismembered corpse has been confidently traced to Alnwick abbey in Northumberland, from where it disappeared, probably at the Reformation. A skull displayed in the Almonry Museum and Heritage Centre at Evesham may belong to a member of the Montfort family. Stories abound, of secret tunnels under the River Avon, and of remains collected by Montfort's widow and interred in St Mary's abbey, Kenilworth.

In this booklet Dr Cox reviews the evidence for an alternative last resting place of Earl Simon's bones, and outlines the circumstances under which they might be recovered and identified. A challenge thus awaits us -- to provide for Simon de Montfort the discovery and preservation accorded to the last Plantagenet king of England, Richard III.

~ David Snowden, Evesham

Preface and acknowledgements

In 1965 the position was chosen for a memorial at Evesham to Simon de Montfort to mark the seven-hundredth anniversary of his death in battle. His mutilated remains were known to have been placed in the abbey in 1265 but evidence from medieval chronicles as to the exact circumstances had not been fully collated. One of them seemed in 1965 to imply that the corpse had been laid to rest immediately in front of the high altar; the new memorial was therefore designed to represent the altar (see the title-page illustration) and was built at its approximate site.[1] Now, however, a wider acquaintance with the relevant sources makes it possible to describe Earl Simon's remains more clearly and to define the grave site more precisely—or rather the sites, for he was buried twice, the second time in a hidden place. Inevitably it will be asked, could the bones now be retrieved, identified, and honourably reinterred, and should they be? This essay does not pronounce on those questions but forms a basis on which they may be discussed.

The arguments presented here were first aired in a lecture that I gave to the Simon de Montfort Society on 13 August 2015. I am grateful to the Society's trustees for supporting its subsequent publication. The following text and notes have been reset, without verbal change, from my article (under the same title) in the *Transactions of the Worcestershire Archaeological Society*, Third Series, vol. XXVI (2018), pp. 159–171, by kind permission of the Archaeological Society and of its Hon.

Editor, Robin Whittaker. The photographs on which Figs 3 and 4 are based were taken by John France of the Worcestershire Archive and Archaeology Service (WAAS) and are reproduced by kind permission of the Vale of Evesham Historical Society. As usual I thank my wife Janice for advice on style and arrangement. David Snowden, of the Simon de Montfort Society, has expertly overseen the design, typesetting, and production.

~ David Cox, Shrewsbury

The first burial

There are two accounts of the blow that killed Earl Simon. A chronicle from Lanercost priory in Cumberland says that '*his armour having been opened at the back, someone plunged his dagger* [sica] *deep into the neck*'.[2] The chronicler may never have been to Evesham but he could have learnt about the manner of Earl Simon's death at second or third hand, having copied the passage from a chronicle written *c*.1297 by a Franciscan friar, Richard of Durham; and Richard may have had the information from someone who fought at Evesham.[3]

Richard of Durham's account seems to be borne out by an anonymous narrative in College of Arms MS 3/23B, in which the corresponding passage is probably also derived from an eyewitness.[4] The surviving copy was made in the early fourteenth century and the passage is somewhat garbled there, but it says that '*with his pointed weapon* [broche] *someone* [verb omitted] *the neck right through*'.[5] Both passages attest to a fatal neck wound from a pointed weapon, and one or more vertebrae may thus have received a cut.

Several medieval chronicles record that Earl Simon's head, hands and feet were cut off on the battlefield after his death and dispersed to various parts of the country.[6] The records seem to imply that the points of amputation were at the neck and below the elbows and knees. There were other blows too. According to the College of Arms narrative, the earl's enemies '*continued to inflict wounds all over the corpse long after it was dead*'.[7] If, in addition to the amputations, the corpse suffered those other injuries, some marks from them may likewise have been left on the bones. Nevertheless, though the earl's corpse lacked head, hands and feet before it was buried, the rest of the soft tissue and of the articulated skeleton supporting it was still mostly present.

The nature of Earl Simon's first grave is described only in the annals of Osney priory near Oxford, which were completed *c.*1277. They say that when the monks brought the corpse from the battlefield they *'wrapped it in a clean linen cloth and laid it in a new tomb* [monumentum], *wherein never yet any man had been laid'.*[8] The statement is factually suspect because it merely copies the biblical accounts of Christ's entombment in a rock-cut chamber. In Matthew's gospel it is said of Christ's body that Joseph of Arimathaea *'wrapped it up in a clean linen cloth. And laid it in his own new monument* [monumentum], *which he had hewed out in a rock'*;[9] Mark says that Joseph *'wrapped him up in the fine linen, and laid him in a sepulchre* [monumentum] *which was hewed out of a rock'*;[10] and in Luke's gospel we read that Joseph *'wrapped him in fine linen, and laid him in a sepulchre* [monumentum] *that was hewed in stone, wherein never yet any man had been laid'.*[11] One cannot therefore safely deduce from the word *monumentum* in the Osney annals that Simon was buried in a stone coffin or tomb or in any coffin at all. A more reliable source, the Evesham collection of the earl's posthumous miracles, which was completed about 1280, usually refers to his first grave by the terms *tumulus* and *tumba*, which it treats as interchangeable;[12] both words can mean either a grave or a tomb.[13]

There are two medieval records of the exact position of Earl Simon's first burial place. One of them is especially useful because it was written by a contemporary monk of Evesham, one who wrote or contributed to the miracle collection. He tells a story that reveals that Earl Simon's first grave had been in the liturgical choir of the abbey church: a deacon from Burton on Trent who had lost his sight came to Evesham about 1280 and there, *'standing in the choir, where the earl had been buried* [sepultus fuerat], *and praying devoutly,* ... *he was given back clear sight'*.[14] The earl's remains 'had been' buried there and were no longer present.

In a medieval Benedictine church the liturgical choir, where the monks sang the daily offices, was usually in the crossing— the place where the four arms of the building met—and over the crossing was usually a central tower; at Evesham the foundations of four piers that supported a central tower were found in the nineteenth century (Fig. 3).[15] The position of the liturgical choir in relation to the central tower is confirmed at Evesham by a contemporary memorandum. It occurs in the margin of a printed bible of 1537 that belonged to Evesham abbey and is now preserved at Evesham in the Almonry Heritage Centre. The bible contains handwritten notes made after the Dissolution by John Alcester one the former monks. There he states that *'there were five bells over the choir and six in the tower'*.[16] One of the sets of bells was in the detached bell tower and was therefore not 'over the choir'. The set of bells that was 'over the choir' must have then been in the other great tower, the central tower of the abbey church. Evidently the liturgical choir was under the central tower and thus in the crossing.

Simon de Montfort's first grave was in the crossing of the abbey church, but that was a large space about forty feet (12m) square (Fig. 1). The annals of the Cistercian abbey of Waverley in Surrey, which were maintained every year until 1266, help one to be more precise. According to the Waverley annalist,

> the bodies of Sir Simon de Montfort and Henry his son and Sir Hugh Despenser were entombed, by leave of the king, in the conventual church of Evesham before the high altar, that is to say lower down before the steps.[17]

In a medieval Benedictine church the high altar was not in the choir but in the presbytery farther east, where the conventual high mass was celebrated. The high altar at Evesham may have stood on a step or steps but they were evidently not the steps referred to in the Waverley annals, because the Montfortian graves, said to have been in front of those steps were, as we have seen, in the choir not the presbytery. When the annalist says 'lower down before the steps', he must mean the steps that rose from the choir to the presbytery and thus to the high altar. There had to be steps in that position because the presbytery was built over a crypt. The crypt was sunk into the earth but its roof—the floor of the presbytery—had to be above ground level so that the crypt could have windows outwards.

As excavation of the crypt in the nineteenth century demonstrated,

> The remains of the western wall of this crypt being above nine feet high, and there being no vestige of any springers for the vaulted roof, proves that the pavement of the choir [i.e. the presbytery] must have been several feet higher than that of the transept [i.e. the transepts and the crossing].[18]

The Rudges' discovery of the western wall of the crypt (Fig. 4) established exactly the former position of the steps up to the presbytery from the crossing.

So Simon de Montfort and two other barons were buried in the choir and just in front of the steps up to the presbytery. In 1265 the crossing space available for those graves was determined by pre-existing features. The north and south sides of the crossing were occupied by the monks' stalls, and in the central space between them stood the tomb of St Wulfsige, a revered hermit, set there more than a century and a half before.[19] There are two references to Wulfsige's tomb being in the choir in the thirteenth century. About 1217 the sacrist Thomas of Marlborough

> *made the lectern at the rear of the choir; which had not been done before in the church of Evesham, but the readings had been read next to the tomb of St Wulfsige.*[20]

And the Evesham liturgy prescribes that the abbot

> *shall enter the choir ... and shall stand there in his stall .... The priest who shall have blessed the water and sprinkled the tomb of St Wulfsige ... shall pass him the sprinkler.*[21]

The lectern, being 'at the rear of the choir', would thus have stood west of Wulfsige's tomb. Earl Simon's first grave had therefore to be placed east of St Wulfsige's tomb, and so just in front of the steps to the presbytery (Fig. 1). The graves of Henry de Montfort and Hugh le Despenser were nearby, but the positions of the three bodies relative to each other are not known.

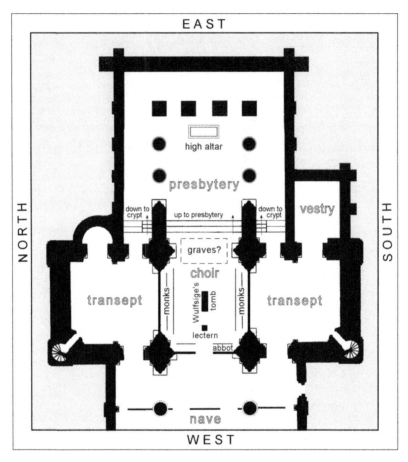

Fig. 1. Reconstruction plan of abbey church (eastern part) in 1265.

If the site of Simon de Montfort's first grave was in front of the presbytery steps, one may ask what was found there when Edward Rudge and his son Edward John uncovered the church between the years 1812 and 1823.[22] In what has been the only attempt to excavate the whole abbey, their aim was '*to ascertain*

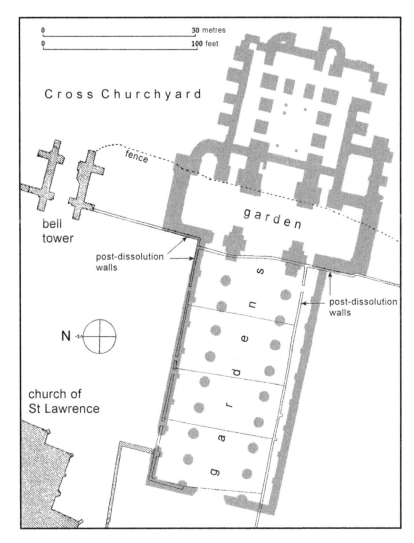

Fig. 2. Excavated remains of abbey church (grey) in relation to surface features. Sources include: Rudge, *Memoir*, pl. LXVII; Ordnance Survey, town plan 1/500, Worcs. XLIX.3.9 (1885 edn).

the site and proportions of the abbey church',[23] and in 1820 Edward John wrote of '*regularly laying down a ground plan of the foundations, as the digging proceeded*'.[24] They were also interested in graves, and several were found, but there is nothing in the Rudges' surviving records, or in Edward John's published report, to suggest that they had thought about finding the grave of Simon de Montfort.[25]

After the Rudges had come to the end of the eastern phase of their excavations they decided to dig the nave before attempting to explore the intermediate and less accessible area, which lay inside a fence[28] and contained most of the crossing and transepts (Fig. 2). Within the fence the Rudges' findings are inconclusive as to burials. Their excavation plan of the whole church, drawn *c*.1824, shows the crossing area as a blank (Fig. 3), but it is inconceivable that there was nothing to be found there except grave 'E'—no trace, for example, of the tomb of St Wulfsige. I therefore think it likely that the crossing was not properly explored. The confined space inside the fence would have been difficult to dig and the Rudges may have had little incentive to complete the task; their excavations had already enabled them to reconstruct the ground plan of the church to their own satisfaction, and it seems that they were not looking for Simon de Montfort's grave or the tomb of St Wulfsige.

In the early nineteenth century the eastern part of the monastic church lay under unenclosed pasture in the Cross Churchyard (Fig. 2). Because it was the easiest part of the church to dig, that is where the first stage of the Rudge excavations took place. During that phase the Rudges found only one burial in the crossing, a wooden coffin next to the north-east crossing

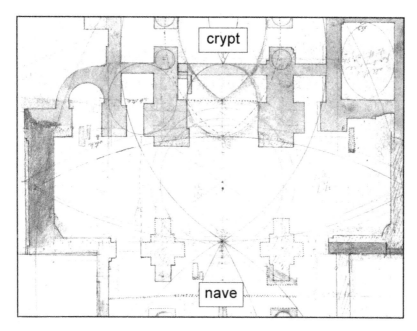

Fig. 3. Extract (crossing and transepts) from abbey excavation plan c.1824. In WAAS, BA 5044/19 Class r899:251 (boxed lettering has been added here).

pier; its position is marked 'E' on their manuscript plan of c.1817 (Fig. 4). It was one of four wooden coffins ('C' to 'F') unearthed in various positions at the western limit of that phase of digging,[26] during which the crypt and the eastern sides of the crossing and transepts were uncovered.

Had coffin 'E' contained recognizable bones, or anything else of interest, E. J. Rudge would presumably have reported them in his usual way, but he mentioned nothing.[27] It appears now that coffin 'E' was not far from the suggested site of Earl Simon's first grave and could conceivably have been his or that

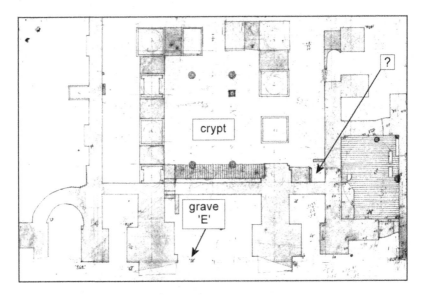

Fig. 4. Extract from eastern part of abbey excavation plan c.1817. In WAAS, BA 5044/19 Class r899:251 (boxed lettering and arrows have been added here).

of one of his companions, Henry de Montfort or Hugh le Despenser. If so, at least two other coffins should have been found near 'E'. That they were not, however, suggests that some graves in front of the presbytery steps were missed by the Rudges, including perhaps that of Earl Simon.

Pilgrimage forbidden

After 1265 Earl Simon's grave might have remained undisturbed in the choir, had it not become a site of popular devotion almost immediately, and an annoyance of the victors of Evesham. Between 1265 and 1280 the abbey recorded about two hundred posthumous miracles performed by Simon de Montfort.[29] Only a fifth of them are said to have involved a visit to Evesham by a sick person or their representative—and then not always to the grave itself, for some went instead to the 'Earl's well' on the battlefield. But every recorded miracle, wherever it occurred, was reported to Evesham abbey and thus implies a visit by someone connected to a supposedly miraculous event. Moreover, the record does not include the pilgrims who came to Evesham and did not experience a miracle, and they must have been the majority; at Lourdes, for instance, pilgrims have far outnumbered the apparent cures. One can hardly avoid the conclusion that hundreds of people, perhaps thousands, came to see Earl Simon's first grave. Their daily donations were so great as to contribute significantly to an expensive building campaign that started at Evesham abbey in 1275. According to Richard of Durham,

> *We have seen many people testify by word of mouth to the signs of healing that they have experienced for themselves; but if men shall keep silent about those signs, let both the daily offerings and the buildings erected there be seen to proclaim them through the stones.*[30]

To Henry III and the Lord Edward, his son, Earl Simon was a justly defeated traitor who at the time of his death was under papal sentence of excommunication. Moreover, his cult was an obstacle to the conclusion of a lasting peace, for parts of England were still at war after the battle of Evesham. Rebels were holding out in several places, and in the country at large there was much sympathy for the Montfortian cause; the miracles were propaganda for all the disaffected. King Henry therefore had an interest in discouraging the miracle stories by having the site of Earl Simon's grave closed down.

The monks of Evesham would have been disinclined to close it themselves because the religious orders had generally supported Simon de Montfort's policies and the pilgrims were now bringing in a lot of money. Moreover, the abbot-elect of Evesham, William of Marlborough, stood directly in the way of closure. The monks had elected him from their own chapter as far back as 1263, but the country had been so disturbed since then that William had been unable to travel to Rome to get papal confirmation of his appointment and Rome had been unable to send a legate to England to grant the confirmation on the pope's behalf.[31] William had therefore never proceeded to being consecrated as abbot and to being formally installed. Nevertheless, he was the senior figure at Evesham abbey at the time of the battle and was now allowing—perhaps encouraging—crowds of pilgrims to visit Earl Simon's grave and spread stories of miracles. Indeed Abbot-elect William had no desire to oblige the king, whose supporters had pillaged his abbey and its town immediately after the battle and had desecrated the abbey church by committing acts of bloodshed within it.[32]

William was no friend of Henry III but the king, having formally approved his election in 1263, did not now have the power unilaterally to bar him from the abbacy. Only the pope or his legate could do it, by withholding confirmation of the election; and as a supporter of King Henry the pope was quite ready to take that step. On 18 June 1266 he instructed his representative in England, the legate Cardinal Ottobuono, to examine the status of William of Marlborough the abbot-elect; if William was found unfit to hold the office of abbot of Evesham, his election was to be cancelled and a fit person appointed.[33] It did not take the legate long to decide that neither William nor any of his monks was suitable for the post. By 15 September 1266 Ottobuono had therefore appointed an outsider to be abbot, William of Whitchurch;[34] he was both experienced and local, having been abbot of Alcester since 1254 and cellarer of Pershore abbey before that.[35]

The next month, on 31 October 1266, the peace terms brokered by Ottobuono between the king and the rebels stipulated that

> *the lord legate shall absolutely forbid, under distraint of the Church, that Simon, earl of Leicester, be considered to be holy or just, given that he died excommunicate according to the belief of the Holy Church. And that the vain and foolish miracles attributed to him by some people, shall not at any time pass any lips. And that the lord king shall agree strictly to forbid this under pain of corporal punishment.*[36]

The second burial

Abbot Whitchurch can have been in no doubt that Cardinal Ottobuono had appointed him on the understanding that he would discourage further pilgrimages to the earl's grave regardless of the effect on the abbey's income. But the new abbot could not be asked to deny people access to the abbey church; the public had a customary right of entry. For instance, the monks had been unable to stop an unwanted visit by their bishop in 1202 because convention required them to leave open *'the gates and entrances of the church where all Christians enter'*.[37] The abbot could, however, remove Simon de Montfort's grave from public view and hope by that means to dampen expectations of new miracles. And that is what he did.

The removal of Earl Simon's remains and the reasons for it are recorded in the Osney annals:

> *After a short interval of time it happened that some of our people, not yet satisfied by the earl's death, murmured and practised yet greater vengeance upon the dead body, saying that it was not worthy of Christian burial, because it was involved in a sentence of excommunication, and because it was infected with the leprosy of treachery. And they endeavoured and prevailed to such an extent that it was disentombed and banished to a more remote place, which place to this day is hidden and unknown except to very few.*[38]

A chronicle from St Albans, written in the early fourteenth century, says that the monks *carried the body of the said earl to their monastery with great reverence and buried it honourably in a very secret place in their abbey, something unknown to everyone for a long time. For they feared to incur the indignation of the great; if they* [the great] *had happened to know them* [the monks] *to have exhibited such grace towards the said earl, they would perhaps have accused them of not a little injuring the king's majesty.*[39]

The St Albans writer, consciously or not, has merged the secret burial with the first, but the Osney annalist makes clear that the secret burial was the second of the two. Nevertheless, the St Albans chronicle is helpful because it states that the remains were not removed from the abbey altogether but were simply taken to a hidden part of it, unknown and unvisited by the public, and interred there in a dignified way.[40]

Abbot William of Whitchurch's strategy of hiding the remains seemed to work as he had hoped: the number of pilgrims started to decline, as did the stories of miracles.[41] Those people who did come to the abbey as pilgrims were allowed only to visit the empty grave that Earl Simon had occupied originally, which was evidently still visible in the crossing of the abbey church.[42] It may seem odd that they should have been attracted by an empty grave, a cenotaph, but that was as near as they could get to Earl Simon himself; and in other churches, too, people revered the empty graves of saints whose remains had been moved, for instance those of Swithun at Winchester, Thomas Cantilupe at Hereford, Thomas Becket at Canterbury, and William of York at the minster.[43]

The search for Earl Simon's remains now shifts from the choir of the church to a hidden place somewhere in the abbey.

But there is no medieval record of where that was. Chroniclers speak only of the monks putting Earl Simon's remains in '*a more remote place, which place to this day is hidden and unknown except to very few*' and '*a very secret place in their abbey, something unknown to everyone for a long time*'.

In an attempt to penetrate the secrecy it may be observed that one Latin word for a hidden place is *crypta*—though it does not occur in the passages just quoted. From the Latin are derived such English words as 'cryptic' and 'encryption', and of course 'crypt'. All of them refer to something hidden or secret, and I believe the secret place in which Earl Simon's remains were finally laid may have been the crypt of the abbey church. It is not known that the public ever had occasion to enter the crypt; the laity sometimes used the nave, and the principal shrines visited by pilgrims were also above ground in the church's eastern arm.[44] Even if one were to find that visitors were occasionally allowed into the crypt, Ranulf Higden, a fourteenth-century chronicler, reminds us that

> *the monks of Evesham, among whom Simon is entombed, dare neither to show the tomb nor to publish the miracles because of fear of the royalists.*[45]

By the sixteenth century one would have descended from the choir to the aisled Norman crypt by a narrow stairway at the north side of the broad steps that rose from the crossing to the presbytery;[46] those narrow steps to the crypt are shown on the Rudges' excavation plan of *c.*1817 (Fig. 4). They were not, however, the steps in use in the early thirteenth century, when directions for one of the services say that

> *The procession shall leave by the lower* [i.e. western] *doorway of the choir ... and they shall turn past the altar of St John the Baptist as far as the entrance to the crypt.*[47]

The position of the altar of St John the Baptist is not known, but the crypt entrance referred to was evidently not in the choir at that time but outside it, beyond its west doorway. Analogy with other monastic churches suggests that the crypt originally had two entrances, by steps descending from the transepts into the west ends of the crypt's side aisles (Fig. 1); that was the arrangement at St Augustine's Canterbury and at Worcester cathedral priory.[48] The stairway that the Rudges found may date only from the rebuilding of the presbytery, which began in 1395.[49]

The Rudges found a number of burials in the nave and a few in the transepts and chapter house, but they found no evidence that the crypt had ever been one of the customary places of burial within the abbey church. The whole crypt seems to have been uncovered during the Rudge excavations: according to Edward Rudge, '*We almost completely made out last year* [1815] *the crypt of the abbey church*';[50] it is depicted in its entirety on the plan of *c.*1817; and Edward John was able to report that '*the floor of the centre aisle had been tiled, and a portion remained at the west end*'; by implication the east end of the aisle had also been uncovered.[51] Nevertheless, they found only one grave in the crypt (arrowed in Fig. 4), in one of the parts of it that would have been least conspicuous to a visitor. Not only was the grave oddly sited but it was of unusual construction. E. J. Rudge described it as follows:

> *Here, in the south-west angle of the crypt, two low walls were built upon the ancient plaster floor, at right angles to each other, forming with the main walls a tomb, containing fine mould and part of a skeleton. This had been disturbed at the dissolution, and must have been the remains of some distinguished personage.*[52]

The description does not specify that the bones lay on the floor, but that would seem to be implied. If so, the burial would not have been a grave in the sense of something dug, but a tomb. From the Rudges' *c.*1817 plan and from their information that the crypt was sixty-nine feet six inches (21.2m) wide,[53] one may calculate that the tomb was internally about six feet (1.8m) long and four feet (1.2m) wide. If there were steps down from the south transept to the crypt's south aisle in the 1260s, there would have been room to insert the tomb next to the steps.[54]

The Rudges did not try to make a connection between the crypt tomb and the remains of Simon de Montfort but several elements of Edward John's description are compatible with such an identification. The remains were 'part of a skeleton'; if they were those of Earl Simon they would indeed have been only part of a skeleton when laid to rest, with no hands, feet, or skull. Moreover, while the Rudges thought that the skeleton had been 'disturbed at the dissolution', Simon de Montfort's remains could also have been disturbed on being removed from the choir. Furthermore the skeleton was assumed to be that of a 'distinguished personage'; only people of social standing could expect to be laid to rest inside the church; and the remains were in a large chest tomb that was unlike anything else found by the Rudges.

Recovery and identification: matters for consideration

If it should be decided to attempt a recovery of the bones of Simon de Montfort, the crypt tomb would, I think, be the most promising place in which to look for them. Such an investigation at Evesham would call for a team in possession of the most advanced techniques and blessed with the degree of luck that attended the exhumation and identification of King Richard III.

A successful excavation of the crypt tomb would depend on closely estimating its present position under the surface. The Rudges' plan of *c*.1817 was drawn at an eighth of an inch to the foot and, in its entirety (Fig. 4 is only a reduced detail), shows the position of the tomb in relation to the cloister arch, which still stands. A surveyor could therefore use the plan to find the approximate place to start digging. Allowance would need to be made, however, for possible inaccuracies in the plan; a small excavation very near the tomb site in 1958 concluded that the *c*.1817 plan of that area was *'in error to the extent of 6 feet* [1.8m] *to the North and 4 feet* [1.2m] *to the West'*, in other words that the remains lay farther south and east than they appear on the *c*.1817 plan. The calculation made in 1958 depends, however, on the excavators having, at the time, correctly identified the small amount of walling that they had uncovered.[55]

The suggested site is under grass in a public park, not close to standing structures, and the presence of underground services is unlikely. Access would therefore seem to be unencumbered, subject only to the appropriate permissions. The tomb rested on the crypt floor, so it cannot be near the present ground surface. E. J. Rudge reported that the floor of the crypt was nine feet (2.7m) lower than that of the 'transept' (in which he included the crossing), and that the floor of the 'transept' was two feet nine inches (0.8m) below the 'floor' of the bell tower.[56] Bearing in mind that the floor of the tower (i.e. the footpath through its archway) was remade and relevelled in 1883,[57] one may say only that the crypt floor could lie somewhere around eleven feet nine inches (3.6m) below that of the tower. Moreover the ground surface between the tower and the tomb site is uneven; an attempt to estimate the vertical distance between the ground surface at the tomb site and the floor on which the tomb was found should also take that into account.

Identification of the bones with those of Simon de Montfort would depend on their present state of preservation. Within the whole church the Rudges found the remains of thirteen skeletons in stone coffins. Edward John reported that '*In those without lids, the bones were covered with lime rubbish, and well preserved*'; in two other stone coffins, however, the bones were decomposed. The remains of thirteen or fourteen wooden coffins were also found in the church but E. J. Rudge mentioned bones in only one of them,[58] which suggests a low level of bone survival in that kind of coffin.

All the bones found in the church were left undisturbed by the Rudges except for a few in which they were particularly interested: from the nave the skull and thigh bones from a stone coffin that they attributed to Abbot Henry (d.1263); also from the nave, a fractured skull from a skeleton with no coffin, which they suggested might have belonged to 'one of the knights who fell at the battle of Evesham'. All of those bones are now in the Almonry Museum and Heritage Centre at Evesham; their condition is sound and Abbot Henry's would be slightly older than any that might have survived from 1265.

The state of the remains in the crypt tomb when the Rudges found them may have been determined not only by the nineteenth-century environment but also by conditions centuries earlier: before the Dissolution the bones had been sheltered by the tomb (though without the inner protection of a stone coffin), and after the Dissolution they had probably been exposed for a time when the tomb lost its cover and before soil had accumulated over them. Nevertheless, the Rudges saw the bones in a condition good enough to allow a description; they were found to have been 'disturbed' but sufficiently whole and connected to be seen as 'part of a skeleton'. The bones may not have decayed markedly since the early nineteenth century, having presumably remained *in situ*.

If the bones were to be recovered, radiocarbon dating of them might then be possible, and that would give a very broad indication of the period in which the death occurred. If the year 1265 fell within that period, the fact would provide further evidence to suggest that the grave was that of Simon de Montfort. Ultimate proof, however, would depend on extracting mitochondrial DNA from the bones, and then matching it with a sample taken from someone who could be proved to have descended in a continuous female line from Earl Simon's mother Alice de Montmorency, or from one of her female ancestors. Those are the processes that were applied successfully by Leicester University to the bones of Richard III.

The task would be long, expensive, and possibly fruitless, involving the participation of specialist laboratories and of scholars competent to find and interpret reliable genealogical records.

The identification of Earl Simon's bones, if it were achieved, would probably add to historical knowledge by confirming and augmenting what we know of his stature, health, death, and burial. Other results might include a deepening of public interest in Earl Simon and the provision of a visible and permanent resting place, but those are objectives for others to consider.

Notes

1   *Evesham Journal*, 29 January 1965.
2   'armis suis a parte posteriori detectis, sicam ejus fundo servulis [? *recte* cervicis] manus impressit': *Chronicon de Lanercost 1201–1346*, ed. J. Stevenson (Bannatyne Club, 1839) [hereafter *Lanercost*], 76. The word *servulis* (the dative or ablative plural of *servulus*, 'a minor servant') seems to make no sense here and is therefore assumed to be a copyist's error; in D. C. Cox, *The Battle of Evesham: A New Account* (Evesham, 1988) [hereafter Cox, *Battle*], 16, I misinterpreted the passage to mean that Simon's killer was 'one of the common soldiers'.
3   A. G. Little, 'The authorship of the Lanercost chronicle', *Franciscan Papers, Lists, and Documents* (Manchester, 1943), 42–54 (at 48).
4   O. de Laborderie, J. R. Maddicott, and D. A. Carpenter, 'The last hours of Simon de Montfort: a new account', *English Historical Review*, CXV (2000), 378–412 [hereafter 'Last hours'] (at 392).
5   'de sa broche lacola par mi': London: College of Arms, MS 3/23B, m. 5d. In the light of Richard of Durham's account, the reading should probably be emended to 'de sa broche le col a [*past participle omitted*] par mi'. In print the MS reading has been rendered as 'de sa broche l'acola parmi' but has been correctly translated as 'with his lance struck him through the neck': 'Last hours', 408, 411.

6   The sources that refer to the amputations are listed in Cox, *Battle*, 38 n. 82. For the dispersal of the severed parts see ibid. 21.
7   'le corps, de pieça mort, de totes parts plaierent': 'Last hours', 408.
8   'in lintheamine mundo involventes, in monumento novo deposuerunt, in quo nondum quisquam positus fuerat': 'Annales monasterii de Oseneia', *Annales monastici*, ed. H. R. Luard, IV (Rolls Series, 1869), 3–352 [hereafter 'Osney'] (at 175–176). On the annals' date of completion see ibid. p. xv.
9   'involvit illud in sindone munda et posuit illud in monumento suo novo quod exciderat in petra': Matt. 27:59–60. In the text of this publication I quote the Douai–Reims translation of the Vulgate.
10 'involvit sindone et posuit eum in monumento quod erat excisum de petra': Mark 15:46.
11 'involvit sindone et posuit eum in monumento exciso in quo nondum quisquam positus fuerat': Luke 23:53.
12 'qui tandem ad tumulum beati Simonis veniens, et, accepto pulvere de dicta tumba, brachium suum fricuit': 'Miracula Simonis de Montfort', *The Chronicle of William de Rishanger of the Barons' Wars. The Miracles of Simon de Montfort*, ed. J. O. Halliwell (Camden Society, 1840), 67–110 [hereafter 'Miracula'] (at 107). The term *sepulcrum* is used once: ibid. 93.
13 *Dictionary of Medieval Latin from British Sources*, fasc. 17, ed. R. K. Ashdowne (Oxford, 2013), 3521, 3523.
14 'stans in choro ubi sepultus fuerat Comes, orans devote … redditus est ei visus perspicuus': 'Miracula', 109. Henry's visit was in or after 1279, the date of the preceding miracle in the collection: ibid. 108.

15 E. J. Rudge, *Memoir, on the Antiquities discovered by Edward Rudge, Esq. F.S.A., F.R.S., F.L.S., in excavating the Ruins of the Abbey Church of Evesham* (Vetusta Monumenta, V [pt 12], 1835) [hereafter Rudge, *Memoir*], 4.

16 'Ther were .v. bellys owere the quere and vi in tha towre': Evesham: Almonry Heritage Centre, 'Matthew's bible', MS note at the end of the Old Testament (illustrated in B. G. Cox, *The Book of Evesham* (Chesham, 1977), 31).

17 'tumulata sunt corpora domini Symonis de Monteforti et Henrici filii sui et domini Hugonis Dispensatoris, per licentiam domini regis, in ecclesia conventuali de Evesham, ante magnam altare, scilicet ante gradum inferius': 'Annales monasterii de Waverleia', *Annales monastici*, ed. H. R. Luard, II (Rolls Series, 1865), 129–411 (at 365). On the annals' date of completion see ibid. p. xxxvi.

18 Rudge, *Memoir*, 4. Rudge used 'choir' in an architectural sense, to mean the eastern arm of the church; and 'transept' to embrace the north and south transepts and the crossing.

19 For Wulfsige see D. Cox, *The Church and Vale of Evesham, 700–1215: Lordship, Landscape and Prayer* (Woodbridge, 2015), 84–85, 175.

20 'fecit lectricium retro chorum: quod prius factum non erat in ecclesia Eueshamie, set legebantur lectiones iuxta tumbam sancti Wlsini': Thomas of Marlborough, *History of the Abbey of Evesham*, ed. and trans. J. Sayers and L. Watkiss, (Oxford Medieval Texts, 2003) [Hereafter Marlborough, *History*], 488 (my translation).

21 'ingrediatur chorum … et stet ibi in stallo suo …. Sacerdos

uero qui aquam benedixerit aspersa tumba sancti Wilsini ... tradat ei aspersorium': *Officium ecclesiasticum abbatum secundum usum Eveshamensis monasterii*, ed. H. A. Wilson (Henry Bradshaw Society, VI, 1893) [hereafter *Officium*], col. 11. On the probable date see ibid. pp. xii–xiii.

22 On the circumstances, chronology, and records of the excavations see D. Cox, 'Evesham abbey: the Romanesque church', *Journal of the British Archaeological Association*, CLXIII (2010), 24–70 [hereafter Cox, 'Romanesque church'] (at 28–31).

23 Rudge, *Memoir*, 2.

24 E. J. Rudge, *A Short Account of the History and Antiquities of Evesham* (Evesham, 1820), 54.

25 Relevant papers may have been lost when the Rudges' Evesham house, Abbey Manor, was gutted by fire in 1894: information from Mr Anthony Rudge.

26 Rudge *Memoir*, 9 and pl. LXVII (at nos. 16–19).

27 Ibid. (at no. 17).

28 G. and T. Demidowicz, *Evesham Abbey Bell Tower: An Architectural and Documentary History* (Evesham, 2015) [hereafter Demidowicz, *Bell Tower*], cover and 32–33, 54. The fence also appears on F. Webb's plan of St Lawrence's parish in 1875 (Worcestershire Archive and Archaeology Service, BA 8392/1 Class x899:251).

29 'Miracula', 67–109. The last recorded miracle but two happened in 1279: ibid. 108.

30 'Vidimus plures viva voce testificari signa sanitatum in se experta; sed et oblationes quotidianae et opera fabricae ibi erectae, idem si homines tacuerint per lapides clamare videntur': *Lanercost*, 77. Cf. 'si hii tacuerint lapides

clamabunt' ('if these shall hold their peace, the stones will cry out'): Luke 19:40. For the building campaign see D. C. Cox, 'The building, destruction, and excavation of Evesham abbey: a documentary history', *Transactions of the Worcestershire Archaeological Society*, 3rd ser. XII (1990), 123–146 [hereafter Cox, 'Building'] (at 128, 130).

31 *Calendar of Entries in the Papal Registers relating to Great Britain and Ireland: Papal Letters*, I, ed. W. H. Bliss (London, 1893) [hereafter *Papal Letters*], 392, 420.

32 D. C. Cox, 'The battle of Evesham in the Evesham chronicle', *Historical Research*, LXII (1989), 337–345 (at 343); 'Last hours', 409.

33 *Papal Letters*, 420.

34 *Calendar of the Patent Rolls: Henry III*, V [ed. J. G. Black] (London, 1910), 638.

35 *The Heads of Religious Houses: England and Wales*, II, ed. D. M. Smith and V. C. M. London (Cambridge, 2001), 18, 42.

36 'Rogantes humiliter tam dominum legatum quam dominum regem ut ipse dominus legatus sub districtione ecclesiastica prossus inhibeat, ne S. comes Leycestrie a quocumque pro sancto uel iusto reputetur, cum in excommunicacione sit defunctus, sicut sancta tenet ecclesia; et mirabilia de eo uana et fatua ab aliquibus relata nullis unquam labiis proferantur; et dominus rex hec eadem sub pena corporali uelit districte inhibere': *Documents of the Baronial Movement of Reform and Rebellion 1258–1267*, ed. R. F. Treharne and I. J. Sanders (Oxford Medieval Texts, 1973), 322.

37 'Porte uero et hostia ecclesie, qua omnes Cristiani ingredi-

untur, aperta erant': Marlborough, *History*, 214.

38   'Post parvum temporis intervallum quidam forte nostrates, nondum nece comitis saturati, murmurabant et majorem adhuc exercebant vindictam in cadavere mortuo, dicentes illud non esse Christiana sepultura dignum, tum quia fuit sententia anathematis innodatum, tum quia fuit proditionis lepra infectum. Et in tantum elaborabant et praevalebant, quod fuit extumulatum et in loco remotiori projectum, qui quidem locus nisi paucissimis usque hodie est occultus et incognitus': 'Osney', 176–177. In 1930 E. F. Jacob mistranslated 'in loco remotiori' as 'into the common sewer': C. Bémont, *Simon de Montfort Earl of Leicester 1208–1265*, ed. E. F. Jacob (Oxford, 1930), 243.

39   'corpus praedicti Comitis ad Monasterium suum, cum magna reverentia, asportaverunt, et honorifice in secretiori loco coenobii sui reconderunt, per multum tempus a cunctis ignotum. Metuebant enim indignationem magnatum incurrere; forte si cognovissent eos tantam gratiam dicto Comiti exhibuisse, imposuissent eis forsan regiam majestatem non modicum laesisse': 'Opus chronicorum', *Chronica monasterii S. Albani*, ed. H. T. Riley [III] (Rolls Series, 1866), 3–59 (at 20).

40   In Cox, *Battle*, 21, I stated incorrectly that the hiding place was 'evidently unconsecrated'. That was a mistaken inference from the complaint of the earl's son Amaury in 1267 that it was not a Christian burial because Simon was still treated as excommunicate: *Les Registres de Clément IV*, ed. E. Jordan, II (Paris, 1894), 139.

41   Cox, *Battle*, 21–22.

42 'Miracula', 106–107, 108–109.
43 J. Crook, 'St Swithun of Winchester', *Winchester Cathedral: Nine Hundred Years 1093–1993*, ed. J. Crook (Chichester, 1993), 57–68 (at 57, 59); J. Crook, *English Medieval Shrines* (Woodbridge, 2011), 236, 260; J. C. Wall, *Shrines of British Saints* (London, 1905), 164–165.
44 Cox, 'Romanesque church', 58–59, 62.
45 'monachi de Evesham inter quos Simon tumulatur propter regium metum, nec tumulum ostendere, nec miracula audent publicare': *Polychronicon Ranulphi Higden monachi Cestrensis*, III, ed. J. R. Lumby (Rolls Series, 1871), 250 n. 18.
46 'Several stone steps leading from the transept [i.e. the crossing] remained *in situ*': Rudge, *Memoir*, 4.
47 'exeat processio per hostium inferius chori … et diuertant per altare sancti iohannis baptiste usque in criptam': *Officium*, col. 57.
48 R. Gem, 'The Anglo-Saxon and Norman Churches', *English Heritage Book of St Augustine's Abbey Canterbury*, ed. R. Gem (London, 1997), 90–122 (at 113, 115); P. Barker, C. Romain, and C. Guy, *Worcester Cathedral: A Short History* (Almeley, 2007), 20–22.
49 Cox, 'Building', 128.
50 Edward Rudge to [Peter] Prattinton, 15 January 1816: London, Society of Antiquaries, MS 520/I [Prattinton Collection, 'Worcestershire Parishes'], vol. XII, p. 492.
51 Rudge, *Memoir*, 5.
52 Ibid. 9 (no. 33).
53 Ibid. 4.
54 The steps did not necessarily descend immediately next to

the outer wall of the crypt aisle as on the conjectural plan in Cox, 'Romanesque church', 36.
55   T. J. S. Baylis, 'Report on Archaeological Excavations carried out in the Upper Abbey Park, Evesham, in April–July, 1958', typescript ([Evesham] 1958; copy in Evesham Library), 2.
56   Rudge, *Memoir*, 4.
57   Demidowicz, *Bell Tower*, 40, 134.
58   Rudge, *Memoir*, 7–9 and pl. LXVII.

The Simon de Montfort Society

The object of the Society shall be to advance the education of the public in the life and times of Simon de Montfort and particularly, but not exclusively, his connection with Evesham and his part in reforming the government of England ...

The Simon de Montfort Society is a heritage and educational charity, founded in 1987, registered in the UK (**Charity Number 1092319**) affiliated to the Battlefields Trust and a member of the Three Battles Consortium. The Society's programme includes regular monthly lecture meetings with an historical theme, visits to sites of particular historical interest, social events, an annual day-school and a traditional wreath-laying ceremony, service and battlefield walk on the weekend nearest to the anniversary of Earl Simon's death at the Battle of Evesham. The Society publishes *The Lion* magazine, its journal and newsletter, three times a year. It also publishes books and leaflets, including Dr Patrick Rooke's biography of Simon de Montfort.

The Simon de Montfort Society seeks to protect and preserve the site of the Battle of Evesham and other places connected with Simon de Montfort. It expands education resources, making them available to students of all ages and to encourage further research into the thirteenth century and arranges visits to places with medieval connections. In December each year the Society holds a St Nicholas Supper.

Please visit: *www.simondemontfort.org*

Printed in Great Britain
by Amazon